Pure Heart and Free Soul
Unique Poetess

Aisha Idris Suleman

BookLeaf
Publishing
India | USA | UK

Pure Heart and Free Soul – A Unique Poetess
© 2021 Aisha Idris Suleman

All rights reserved.

No part of this publication may be reproduced, stored in a retrieval system, or transmitted, in any form or by any means, electronic, mechanical, photocopying, recording or otherwise, without the prior written permission of the presenters.

Aisha Idris Suleman asserts the moral right to be identified as author of this work.

Presentation by *BookLeaf Publishing*

Web: www.bookleafpub.com

E-mail: info@bookleafpub.com

ISBN: 9789358364309

First edition 2021

"I dedicate this book to my late father (1956 - 2020), who has always taught me to be a strong and independent woman, which I am today. I would also like to dedicate this book to my beautiful son, who is my main source of motivation!

I dedicate this book to each and every one of you, as I do not know what you may be going through in the current timings, but I hope my poems bring a touch of sparkle to your lives!"

Acknowledgements

Those that I love know that I love them! I want to express my special thanks of gratitude to all my readers, who truly enjoy my poems and appreciate each and every word I express. I would also like to thank my late father, who always pushed me to thrive and excel in everything I do, including writing.

Most of all, I want to thank BookLeaf Publishing for giving me the golden opportunity to undertake the writing challenge and showcasing my talent to the world!

Preface

I started writing from a very young age and have achieved numerous awards and recognition for different pieces of work. I have always been passionate about poetry and the feelings that come with it. I see poetry as a form of therapy, as it helps me to express my feelings through words. I do not follow any strict rules or structures when I write and you will see in this book how I write freely and straight from the heart. I love to play with words and although it can take time to come up with a unique piece, the final outcome is always a positive one.

As you read through my poems in this book, you will notice how I love to get my voice across. They say I am the 'voice for the voiceless,' which is true, as I enjoy writing on topics and issues that are currently circulating in the world. I also enjoy motivating and inspiring others through my poems, as it gives my audience a glimpse of hope and encouragement to strive and live life to the fullest. My poems are a source of energy and they will surely uplift your energy and mood!

In addition to this, you may find some of my poems humorous. I enjoy putting a smile on everyone's face as I feel life is too short to be sad or to regret things that are linked to the past. After my father passed away from Covid-19 in April 2020, I felt that life is moving quickly and you can never envisage what will happen, as things do not go according to plan at times. I started to write more poems during the lockdown, as many people were struggling to cope with the pandemic and needed support in one way or the other. It was also an opportunity for me to escape into my own world of imagination!

Similar to my life, I do not like to make my poems complicated, so you may notice whilst reading through them that I do not use a lot of 'fancy' or 'hard to pronounce' words. I like simplicity, as I feel my audience should be able to enjoy reading, without having to look up words that they may not understand. That is why they call me 'a unique poetess,' as there is only one of me! This process can be challenging at times, but the best way to go by is to get different people to proof-read the poems to see if they are able to make sense of it and whether they understand the motive behind it.

I hope you indulge yourself into my poems and remember, a pure heart and a free soul is all you need!

Aisha Idris Suleman

1. BLACK LIVES MATTER

Black lives matter

Stop the shatter

And the violent scatter

The feeling of gutter

With disgust and batter

No praise and flatter

We should know better

This poem is a letter

To avoid the bitter

Brightening hearts with glitter

Black lives are not litter

I am not a quitter

Find me on Instagram and Twitter

Similar to a transmitter

I am a peace fitter

And a hate stripper

Let me give the quiver

My voice like a flowing river

Stop making Black lives dimmer

They have hope to shine and shimmer

They are like you and I, no need to differ

Discontinue acting like you are higher or bigger!

2. FREE PALESTINE

Stop this catastrophic war

Affecting children and the poor

Corpses lying on the floor

I cannot take it anymore

So much blood has been shed

Innocent families have been shred

Buildings put on fire without dread

Do you think this is a way to move ahead?

Let us help the people of Palestine

They have a dream to rise and shine

Stop treating them like a piece of chine

Let them live their lives like yours and mine

FREE PALESTINE, as the phrase speaks

They have put up with so much in these last weeks

I hope you understand my thoughts and shrieks

No more killing, firing, shooting or squeaks!

3. HATRED

Why is there so much hate?

The world needs love of heavy weight

People are losing their faith

And scared to jump out of their wraith

Religion, ethnicity and culture are a label

We are all linked together like a cable

Why can't we all be one?

And fill each other's life with fun

It does not matter what your race

Or the colour of your face

We are in this world together

Walking through the stormy weather

Forget pointing out differences

So we can be in more appearances

Bury this hatred deep down

Or we will be left with a frown

Hatred is a disaster

Similar to an unhappy master

It fills us up with sorrow

And diminishes the beautiful tomorrow!

4. MIND MATTERS

Life is a challenge

Full of average gallons

Each day can be difficult to pass by

With a positive and indifferent eye!

Stress flinches as soon as I wake up

Even before embracing miracle like a cup

Often in thought, my mind goes up and down

Never a smile, just a dreadful frown!

Each minute, I feel a solid burden

Since life is tough and uncertain

It feels like a billion souls weighed upon me

Even though one day, I will firmly break free!

There is no end to any issue or frustration

Ever since my mind feels such temptation

Life is filled with lies, pains and sorrows

But out of the upheaval, comes hardiness for tomorrow!

5. STAY STRONG

Hold your head high

Ability to reach the sky

No looking behind

Just a stress-free mind

Face the hurdles

Travelling in circles

Forget the fears

Wipe away those tears

Listen to yourself

Not someone else

It is your freedom and life

Ignoring each and every strife

Be the strong one

Unique like none

Make it work

Joys of affliction lurk

Anything is possible

Change is no obstacle

Do your thing

You have control of that wing!

6. FLY WITH ME

Come and fly with me

You will be able to see

Beautiful colours of this world

That have gradually unfurled

Come and fly with me

Open your eyes with this key

Discover the charms of nature

And every happy living creature

Come and fly with me

Let it out and be free

So many opportunities arising

Is it not abundantly surprising?

Come and fly with me

Your face lit with impish glee

Having fun all day around

Keeping our feet off the ground

Come and fly with me

You will look back and see

The right steps were taken

Making you now wide awaken!

7. KEEP TRYING

There are times when you will fall

And bang your head against the wall

Some doors will close for good

Even though we did the best we could

Many obstacles will appear your way

The aim is to not let them stay

Pull yourself together and keep trying

Tell yourself it is not worth dying

Keep pushing yourself to reach your aim

Fate will come to you with fame

Believe in your abilities and soul

Your dreams are beyond your control

Some hardships are a real test

Neither of us could do what is best

You have tried virtually everything

Similar to tying scissors to a string

Laugh your way through the problem

Because everybody starts from the
bottom

Have faith and certainty in the power of
God

Show the world that you can overcome
a trembling trod!

8. SMILE

I am going to make you smile

Help you go that extra mile

It does not cost anything

Outfly the bird with your super wing

Smiles are completely free

Try it, at least for me

Your worries and stress will end

Because you have me as your good friend

Don't hide your beautiful smile

Similar to paperwork in a file

Let it take over your burden

And cover it up behind the curtain

Don't forget to wear a smile everyday

Looking like twenty shades of ray

It will make your days and nights better
All the way from January to December!

9. LOVE IS BLIND

Love is a beautiful flower

Just like a relaxing warm shower

It does not matter what the gender

You just have to happily surrender

Feelings cannot be hidden away

Is this not what you wanted me to say?

No need to be scared of the world

As long as you are in my arms, nicely
curled

It does not matter what the age,
ethnicity and sex

Because love is not about being
complex

You just need to have devotion and trust

Otherwise you will never be able to
adjust

Go on, express your beautiful feeling

So I can understand what you are
dealing
I belong to you, without any doubt
Just don't forsake or sell me out!

10.   MOVE   TO   THE RHYTHM

Let's just live it up

Like an icy crystal cup

Whether sad or happy

Or just feeling snappy

Let's move and shake

And wriggle like a snake

There is no right or wrong

Never weak, but always strong

Move to the rhythm

Blinded by the vision

Hear the sound and beat

Giving that ooze and heat

Shake off your body

Similar to a hot toddy

It will free your mind

Leaving stress miles behind!

11. SPRING'S PARADISE

As the Earth's alignment is tilted towards the Sun…

And the number of daylight hours increase…

The trees put forth new leaves…

Making nature look exquisite and at peace!

In the early morning, we hear birds chirping in trees…

The cuckoos' sweet notes captivating us…

The bees' hum filling our souls with delights…

Prompting that Spring is here, so banish the gloomy gus!

It is enchanting to walk through cornfields during Spring…

The green plants flutter in the breeze…

The Earth wears a magnificent green garment…

Which makes our minds feel at ease!

Spring transforms the Earth into paradise…

Making us forget wariness and sorrow…

Inspiring us to use our eyes to see pleasurable sights and ears to hear melodious notes…

As well as encouraging our minds and souls to look forward to the morrow!

12.   LET IT GO

Let those grudges go

The world needs a glow

Life is too short

Let's be each other's support

No point being angry or sad

Let it go and be glad

So much to look forward to

Rather than sitting and feeling blue

Ups and downs are normal

Don't be too formal

Close your eyes and lean back

No need to paint that heart black

Hold onto those that love you

Keep them close to your view

So there is no regret later

Nor feelings of a hater

Forget being so arrogant

Maybe just a little extravagant

Smile and release yourself

Take your soul off the shelf!

13.   CHEER UP

You will feel better

Like salt and pepper

I will make you laugh

As well as your staff

Dressing like a clown

To get rid of your frown

Bouncing up and down

Through the entire town

Having an exciting pillow fight

In the darkness of the night

Forget your tension and worries

And just stay free of the hurries

Life is too short to be sad

Ignore those that treat you bad

Because you are a precious gold

A diamond that I can for sure hold

So cheer up and keep smiling

Grip me and let's continue flying

Not letting obstacles block the fun

Let it unfold steadily, no need to run!

14.   EYES   DO   THE TALKING

Eyes do all the talking

Whether sleeping or walking

Great feelings it can express

No need to verbally confess

Can be serious or naughty

Eyes are that part of body

Maybe humble or haughty

No two pairs can copy

Eyes have a strong power

To please you like a flower

Bringing out the inner soul

Some of which you can't control

Eyes can easily be read

Regardless of thoughts in the head

Moods that cannot be hidden

Whether it is adults or children

So let the eyes talk

And just let it unlock

What you need to say

Without letting words play!

15.   PUT YOUR HANDS UP

Just put your hands up

Like free-flowing tea in a cup

All blissful and careless

And being very zealous

Walk through without worries

Imagine a land of kebab and curries

Blending your inner soul with joy

Similar to a child delving in their toy

Enjoy every second of breath

Live it up fully before death

Do all the things that bring satisfaction

Especially those for which you have
passion

People will say all sorts

And try to make contorts

But don't let it get to you

Just do what you want to do

So put your hands up in the air

Dance like you don't really care

Live your life outside the square

Remember, there is no time to spare!

16. ARROGANCE

Being arrogant is the worst behaviour

It is not an ideal quality for saviour

Thinking you are always right and the best

Maybe it is time to take a real test

Why behave unpleasantly towards others?

Trying to shove people under covers

It is a sign of losing contact with the reality

Because you seem to be living in your own fantasy

Having a foolish pride and feeling superior

Making others feel lower in position and inferior

Pause for a moment and look at yourself
in the mirror

The camouflage of insecurity is getting
nearer

There is so much I can be arrogant
about

But I dislike this trait and have kept it out

Don't let arrogance diminish your true
self

It is a killer that will leave you alone on
the shelf!

17.　LOVE YOURSELF

Love yourself more than anything

Because you know the notes to sing

Treat yourself with spoils or a special treat

Flutes play calm music with vanilla apple heat

Take time out and do the little things you love

Watching the hills below and the skies from above

Whether it is bathing, yoga, movies or reading

Your inner soul needs good care and feeding

Even ten minutes a day will keep you motivated

Don't make your life stressful and
extremely complicated

Take this time to forget the world and
focus on yourself

Don't be like a hidden book placed at
the back of a shelf

So look in the mirror and give yourself a
cuddle

Because there is no need for a huge
huddle

Always remember that you are a
diamond

That is the most unique and priceless in
the island!

18. BOOM BOOM BOOM

Hear my heart go boom boom boom

Similar to fragments of lava that fume

Spreading laughter and love with passion

And always dressing in style plus fashion

Hear my heart go boom boom boom

Just forget all the pain and gloom

Spread your wings and fly across the sky

No need to feel embarrassed or shy

Hear my heart go boom boom boom

Don't lock yourself up in the back room

Get out there and show your true colours

Don't compare yourself to others

Hear my heart go boom boom boom

Motivating and inspiring with a zoom

Helping people with a light of positivity

Doing the things I love with proclivity

So hear my heart go boom boom boom

I have been like this from my mother's
womb

Like my father, head up high and
fearless

Circumventing all the worries and
stress!

19.   SURPRISES

Shocking surprises life can bring

Without giving a chance to sing

Some good ones and some sad

Making you happy or really mad

Some people may come and go

Similar to the stream of river flow

You continue searching for them

Only if they were a priceless gem

Anything can happen at anytime

But sometimes it feels like a crime

When you don't know what is coming

There is no chance of hiding or running

Surprises that create twists and turns

Some can be assuring, others full of
concerns

You have to be prepared for all the ups
and downs

Maybe with some laughter or grin and
frowns

Surprises are surprises and they will
remain

Whether there is sun, wind, snow or rain

It is part of life and you must live with it

Just don't think negatively or ever quit!

20. **WHENEVER I SEE YOU AGAIN...**

Whenever I see you again

Whether there is sun or rain

I promise you won't feel the same

You want to tie me with a chain

I will make you forget your pain

And you will want me to remain

In your life's headlong train

My honour is free from stain

The flower is budding fain

The street ahead has become a lane

I don't know how to explain

Do you want to be my friend?

Take a deep breath and count to ten

Let's do it together then

Clutch me tightly like a pen

Trust me, don't confuse your brain

I promise I am here for you until the end!

44